"I'm Left and I'm Right!"

MINDSTIR MEDIA

Published by Mindstir Media, LLC
45 Lafayette Rd | Suite 181| North Hampton, NH 03862 | USA
1.800.767.0531 | www.mindstirmedia.com

Printed in the United States of America
ISBN-13: 978-1-7352710-6-4

"I'm Left and I'm Right!"

The Pocket Handbook
for Progressives©

A Political Parody

John F. Riddell, Jr.

"I'm Left and I'm Right"
The Pocket Handbook for Progressives©

Foreword

Perhaps you have heard of the recent surreptitious discovery of a heretofore top-secret handbook. The booklet apparently has been widely circulated among Progressive Democratic Party operatives and is rather explicit in its guidelines for use. This confidential information was forwarded to me by a former card-carrying member of the book's Pocket Progressive Democrats. This fellow is now hiding out in a box of uncounted ballots somewhere in the swamps of Florida.

With all due respect to the author of the original <u>Screwtape Letters</u>, C.S Lewis, this tome is not intended to demonize in any way any individual, group, or political party. But to paraphrase the words of that effective protector of individual freedom, Mr. Johnny Cochran, if the lies, deception, and criminal acts fit, you must convict.

The booklet is organized around an alphabetical listing of certain words and catchphrases complete with instructions for use and inherent meaning for the faithful zealots. The following is the reproduction of the original manuscript as conveyed to me in a plain manila envelope wrapped in brown shipping paper. Having originally been cautioned about the dangers of unprotected handling of this material, I was warned that the pages of the booklet are coated with an anti-Trump concoction, one that causes the eyes to water, the nose to sneeze, and the skin to itch--but only for President Donald Trump supporters. Despite tearing up, uncontrollable sneezing, and the maddening requirement to scratch that which itches, I have persevered to bring you the following. Please be aware, there is no physical danger to the reader.

The Pocket Handbook for Progressives©

"I'm Left and I'm Right"--Words for Every Progressive to Live By

Please Note: Your first responsibility to the Party is to deny any and all connections or references to the existence or use of this booklet.

"General Guidelines for the Faithful"

We know that we are in a constant battle for the souls and pocketbooks of the American voters. While we have made great strides in these last few years in establishing a solid foothold through the co-opting of our education system, we must press on to take full advantage of this instructional malfeasance. Therefore, these wrongly taught minds will be conducive and supportive of our cause through the careful use of pre-conditioned terms and phrases, strategies and tactics. Use these whenever and wherever possible and never, ever feel the need to explain or justify yourself.

Sincerely,
Your Progressive Leadership Who Always Knows Better Than You

To be an effective acolyte, you must understand our language. With this in mind, we are pleased to provide the following for your reference:

Words to Live By—
A Pocket Dictionary.

"A -C"

Antifa: These seemingly innocent young minds are among our most useful idiots. While they mistakenly think that we agree with them, their mayhem, intimidating, and illegal activities against conservatives and others are just what the always right Rev. Alinsky ordered. They take all the risks; we get all the gain. Defend them at all times until the time comes to stop—then disown them for the real little fascists that they are.

Ballot Harvesting: A definition and an important new tactic. What could possibly be wrong or illegal with our loyal supporters being willing to pick up, collect, drop off, and even mark ballots for unfortunate supporters who could not physically exercise their right to vote? Voter fraud is something we would never tolerate and anyone who accuses us of such action is simply lying. Our mission is to protect voting rights and win our elections and this approach insures that.

Bill of Rights: Certainly, you are aware that this arcane structure was initially written to protect the individual from the government. Our misguided founding fathers wanted to protect the citizens from the very source of protection—our Party running our Government! We must promote this fact. How else can we champion, promote, and institute our "government is the solution" power platform?

Civility: This is to be used to always paint us as the peaceable ones. This can only be accomplished when people wholeheartedly agree with us, therefore it is up to you to emphasize that anyone who disagrees with us is, by our definition and not subject to questioning, uncivil. We need to make sure that voters always believe that civility, not policy, is our main goal. We want the saps to believe that 'Everyone just needs to get along' while we self-righteously pick their pockets.

Climate Deniers: One of our easier targets. Our accomplices in the national media do not even require us to debate senseless topics with facts. As a result, anyone not agreeing with our apocalyptic vision of an ending of all human life 100 years out cannot possibly argue with our perspective that only an all-powerful, central government controlled by Progressive Socialists can fix this "problem." Anyone with the timidity to challenge us is immediately branded a public heretic, an enemy of mankind, a threat to all children. It is, effectively, our license to steal.

CO2 Emissions: Our well-paid scientists-on-the-take have done a fantastic job in promoting the evils of carbon dioxide emissions. They have painted a picture of humanity's future demise in such a way, lifespans being what they are, that no one today could ever prove us wrong. Actively couple this with the promotion of an obvious tax opportunity and a large central government as the only way to reverse the previously outlined demise. This is, indeed, one of our greatest achievements. As CO2 is the natural bi-product of breathing, just think how much money we will get just by taxing for breathing. We'll say we are only going to tax rich breathers, but eventually everyone will pay. Once again, do not let facts to the contrary get in the way of this dogma.

Compromise: Our key position when discussing the intransigence of anyone who opposes us. Internally, we always refer to this as "when the other side caves." Our definition of compromise is "never compromise." Maintain this perspective and never miss the opportunity to use it to describe our willingness to "meet" the unreasonable demands of the other side. Equally important, never actually perform this act of retreat unless it is over some meaningless topic in which case you want to highlight it all out of proportion to its actual relevance. Our media friends are very good at this.

"D-F"

Deflect: Please never forget, thanks to our allies in the media, that we always enjoy the "luxury of gibberish." This is a powerful benefit knowing that whatever we choose to say, regardless of whether we answer the question or counter-dodge a fact, we do not have to make sense. We will never be held accountable! Just say what you want and keep moving forward.

Deniers: Anybody or any organization that disagrees with our "facts" is, by our conscious decision, in denial. Whether dealing with climate, the economy, immigration, etc., people falling into this category are to be criticized based solely on their position being one of immorality. Their opposition to our point of view is counter to all that is right and good and is therefore immoral in the eyes of all mankind. The beauty of this argument is that there is no short defense (see **Racism**), therefore, given the limited attention span of our followers, there is no room (or need) for an objective rebuttal. If you can hang this sign on an opponent, you are already half-way home to winning the battle.

Distraction: (see **Deflect**). Whenever we or our Progressive/Socialist policies are attacked, never fall victim to an attempt at a rational policy discussion. Rather, say that this attack is an obvious and blatant attempt by the racist opposition to direct the public's focus from the core of the real issues, those defined by us.

Due Process: An "old white male" privilege standard for discriminatory action. Now that we have succeeded with having folks accept the premise that any male accused in any sexual misconduct is always guilty until proven innocent, we must expand this logic to cover anybody we deem unacceptable to us. Just remember, "Justice" is how we choose to define it.

Entitlement: Our mechanism for the sustainable solicitation and recruitment of new voters. By promising the world but consistently delivering only a small portion of the promise, we instill and install a personal voter dependency that few would vote to terminate. Therefore, we insure a dependable, if not reluctant, unthinking choice for every ballot. When we wrap this approach in the blankets of social justice with reparations and white privilege, people not only enjoy the crumbs, but they feel good about eating them. We have hit the mother lode—our voters accept our handouts and feel good about themselves and us for making these crumbs available. Why would they ever vote us out and therefore eliminate their crumbs? Our challenge is to just to keep coming up with more crumbs!

Fake News: What the opposition regularly calls our propaganda. With the help of our Media propaganda wing, we have an obligation to tell the American public, not the truth, but what we believe they need to hear. (see **Deniers, Distraction, Deflect**).

Family Values: Make no mistake! This is the most serious threat to our existence. We cannot tolerate these. Remember, our family is the world. Personal history, family history, support of values supporting these two points are nothing more than cultural smokescreens thrown up to hide historical malfeasance. These serve no purpose for those of us dedicated to promoting equality of results. (see **Entitlement, Victimization, White Privilege**).

Fascist: Never worry about knowing what this term actually means. Few of our friends in the media understand the term and even fewer voters know (or care) (see **Antifa**). Just always use it against our opponents! It is one of those terms that, once attached to an individual or group, is an automatic non-detachable negative. The beauty is that our opponents will always spend a tremendous amount of energy and dollars to avoid or counter this tag and all of this effort is basically wasted, ineffective. Never forget—we control the communication pipeline. We can bleed their publicity coffers dry! **Deflect, deflect, deflect**.

Fees and Taxes: We all know that our central government programs require money, and a lot of it, for successful implementation. Unfortunately, the vast majority of our potential contributors have a built-in psychological resistance to the concept of increased taxation. While our education/indoctrination program still has some challenges, one of our great education achievements has resulted in a vast majority of marks not recognizing an increase in their contribution when they see it. This is the result of our clever use of the word "fee" instead of "tax." For us the result is the same, more money to fund our voter solicitation/recruitment programs (see **Entitlement**) with none of the blowback associated with taxes.

For the Children (FtC): Always a safe haven in any debate or argument. This emotional tug allows us to always shift (see **Deflect**) any argument away from factual discussion to an emotional safe space. Anyone who argues with this position does so knowing that our friends in the media will expose them for the heartless souls that they are. Again, we have no need to wallow in the swamp of facts. Our children deserve only our best efforts, not our best arguments!

"G-I"

Green: Our "pro" default position when discussing any public policy impact with any connection to the environment. If it involves any existing carbon-based energy, including but not limited to production or utilization, it is, by our definition, not green. Therefore, in the interest of preserving the planet, we must in good conscience, oppose it. The only force strong enough to combat the ongoing destruction of the planet is the Federal Government. Therefore, all our initiatives must be in strengthening this bulwark against those that would poison our environment and use up our limited resources. To fund this requirement requires our demanding of increased funds through taxes and fees to begin to reverse the pattern of destruction wrought by corporate America.

Hate Speech: We are the protectors of everyone and anyone who hears something that they do not like or find offensive. While we are proud supporters of free speech, we are totally against hate speech. Our power resides in the following sentiment: "We support free speech, but are against hate speech. Who decides what is or is not hate speech? We do!" If what is being said offends you, then by our definition it is founded on hatred (see **Victimization**).

Impeach: One of our best rallying cries. Usually most effective when loudly shouted three times in rapid succession. To be hurled at every government official who disagrees with us. It matters absolutely not a whit the offenses being accused. Our zealots will feed off our self-righteous indignation and the low-level info voters will feed off our zealots. Above all, always remember, we are doing this in defense of our country but also remember that this defense must first be in line with our Party's objectives.

Intersectionality: Not one of our desirable topics. As you undoubtedly know, this term refers to competition among victims as to who is the most victimized (see **Victimization**). Our position has to be that all victims are precious and victimization is always the result of historical white male oppression. If we manage this properly, we should be able to milk enough funds to cover every victim.

"J-O"

Nationalism: This is a great opportunity for us and supports our not-so-visible globalist agenda. Where in the past, our opponents associated this with patriotism, again, thanks to our success in malicious educating, we can now attach this emotion to an extremist position, one held by racists and domestic terrorists (see previous note on **Civility**). Our friends in the media will continue their support of our initiative in this regard by referring to any and all acts of racial or religious intolerance as being solely in the realm of the "white nationalist." Never call attention to anti-Semitic remarks made by members of our Progressive Party such as the Rev. Louis Farrakhan (aka Louis X), Rev. Jeremiah Wright, Rev Jesse Jackson, and Rev Al Sharpton. Completely disavow at every opportunity any factual connection to the Ku Klux Klan or Jim Crow segregation. Just dismiss this as the "past" and quickly move on. Never worry about bad press in this regard. The National Media is our friend."

NRA: Probably our greatest organizational threat and opponent. These people try to get you to believe that their defense of the misguided 2nd Amendment is the foundation of all defenses of the entire Bill of Rights. You must know and accept that this is simply a defense of **Nationalism** and **White Privilege** while supporting **Victimization** and the main obstacle to your personal realization of your desires and **Entitlement**s. Thankfully, leaders in California have deemed this organization and its members as domestic terrorists. It is your duty to act accordingly!

Natural Rights: Ostensibly these are obligations other humans have to provide for the wants of other humans. If there is something that an individual wants then it is only natural that someone else should give it to him or her. (see **White Privilege, Social Justice**).

"P-U"

Racist: Surpassing Fascist as a most powerful label, one that our opponents will do almost anything to avoid being tagged. It is totally unimportant whether the actions and the offending individual actually conforms to the definition of racism. All that matters is that the offender is accused of such activity or attitude. The key here is for our interpretation and accusation to be framed in such a way that is not based on any requirement for objective information or evidence. Rather, we only need subjective innuendo with the support of our media partners to suffice.

Ransack: Whenever the opposition takes funding away from one of our projects. When our dedicated funds are either reduced or re-directed, by our definition, this is immoral, an act of social and political barbarism. (see **Distraction**).

Sanctuary Cities: Who with a heart would ever deny someone the opportunity to a better life for themselves and/or their families? If we believe that open borders are natural rights, then protection for those who exercise this right is the only moral course of action. City services are the only way to provide the humane treatment for these victims of white privilege and social injustice.

Second Amendment: You already know that this is about guns and the misguided perception by our enemies that they somehow have a right to own one. We only support guns for those protecting us against those whose guns we want to take. Remember, people do not kill people, guns do.

Socialism: Do not get bogged down in the traditional, academic definitions. Simply realize that this approach insures that you and your fellow travelers are entitled to all the good things that life has to offer, the good things that you do not have, yet see others who do, the good things that you never should have to work for. (see **Entitlement**)

Social Justice: One of most effective wedges. (See **Victimization**). This allows us to positively address any and all perceived grievances against any group for possible reparations. The key here is to ensure that the perpetrators of any and all grievances are always linked to white males, the older the better. Do not worry. With every passing year the sheer number of these folks who can oppose us at the ballot box, are able to counter our accusations, decrease through natural attrition. We'll just simply outlive them!

Technology: Always a funding factor we can initially support. More is always better. Just remember, unlike a completed physical barrier such as a wall, technology can always be defined and described as an unknown or unproven yet certainly a "better" solution for whatever we define as a priority. (see **Green**)

The American Dream: Any hint or promise of equality of opportunity was intentionally set up by the Founding Fathers to solely benefit white Christians. We and our followers were totally left out of the social, financial, and economic benefits if we did not fit their white

Christian template. As such, we are owed for this abomination of history. We are owed for this absence of justice and equality (See **Victimization, Social Justice**). As white male Christians primarily benefitted, then justice dictates that white male Christians should be expected to pay.

Tolerance: We should always expect and, indeed, demand this from our opponents. Because we have been historically subjected to their biases and oppression, we are owed the debt of forbearance. We, however, have no requirement to reciprocate. Quite to the contrary, our history of their oppression entitles us to never be required to be tolerant of their views which, by definition, contrast or conflict with ours. (see **Entitlement, Victimization, White Privilege**)

Tweets: The most malicious and evil tool used by our arch enemy. Because we cannot control this direct threat to the messaging of our communication wing, the media, we must seize every opportunity to criticize, demean, cast aspersions upon, and just generally condemn this channel. Words such as unpresidential, unprofessional, mean spirited, and the like all support our goal and desire to have this threat to our messaging completely eliminated. (see **Fake News, Hate Speech**)

"V-Z"

Victimization: Probably our single most effective code word. With proper use of this simple word we can remove any responsibility for undesirable outcomes for any and all actual and potential voters. Therefore, the promotion and acceptance of this state of mind ensures that these targets will always support us as long as they believe we will get them something for their newly learned pain and suffering. The beauty of this is with just a little creative thinking on your part we can throw out a big enough net to ensnare just about everyone into feeling that they are a victim of something. Just think of the allegiance, votes, and money this will generate!

White Privilege: Pertains primarily to Caucasian males, generally the older the better. Refers to their position they have attained in their life based primarily on the fact that they were simply born as males and Caucasian (see **Social Justice**). As a result of this unfairness of life, we who are not white and not male are owed and entitled to a debt stemming from this privilege of caste. (see **Entitlement**)

The Progressive Dress Code

Never forget that you are a proud member of an army, an army whose destiny it is to fundamentally change the nature of mankind. As with every army, it is important that you distinguish yourself and your cohorts from others and that is usually by way of a uniform. We also employ a uniform, one most commonly referred to by the uninitiated as a hoodie.

Now this hoodie may be of any color of your choosing but we seriously suggest either black or dark Navy. Clearly, these colors tend to hide any spilled coffee, energy drinks, ketchup, or taco sauce. Under no circumstances dress out in white. We detest any reference to a racial privilege of this color and abhor any and all references to snowflakes. So white is out! Also, we prefer hoodies made only of non-GMO cotton. However, if this is not available, protesting by using polyester will suffice.

This leads us to the second question regarding your uniform—pull-over or zip-up? Now this really boils down to a question of pocket compatibility/coordination underscored by political philosophy. Some folks shy away from having to make the difficult decision of which pocket, the left or the right, should they put their keys, cellphone, Handbook and Pocket Dictionary, etc. Some feel that, given their leftist leanings, only the Handbook should go into the left pocket, while those symbols of capitalism should only go into the right one. Others feel that by putting their Handbook in their right pocket, they are making an anti-establishment statement 24/7. With their keys and other toys in their left pocket, they feel that they are clearly demonstrating their disassociation and dissatisfaction with the status quo. Just remember, at the end of the day, it is your choice—just be sure that you have thought deeply about it, discussed it with your community of friends, and are emotionally at peace with it.

Now what about the all-encompassing kangaroo pocket of the pull-over? For many, this choice frees up their mind from all non-progressive thoughts. Without having to make conscious decisions about which pocket offends society the most, they take comfort in believing that anything that they choose to put into that pocket is an offense to society. Without having to utilize limited brain power for categorizing, all that power can be better focused on changing the world.

Now it also is important that you note a few other attributes of your hoodie. The hood itself can and should always be used to deny any outside cameras a clear picture of your face. In addition, when engaging in crowd sourcing of fruits, vegetables, and food in general, every mob can simply load up their fellow progressive free food fighters' hood with whatever they can get their hands on and no one need even break stride. In addition, this tactic allows anyone who is caught and accused of stealing or shoplifting to rightfully state that they never even touched the items in question.

Now most hoodies also come with strings that surround the facial opening of the hood itself. While these strings can certainly be useful in cinching down the facial opening in an effort to keep warm, their real benefits lie in other areas. Perhaps first and foremost is their role in the relief of anxiety. Please be aware, progressive soldier, that you may well find yourself in situations of great stress. Casually chewing on one of the strings, particularly the right one, has been proven to be a tremendous stress reliever. Simply tying them and untying them repeatedly has also been shown to be a great way to pass the time in the pokey wagon. One pokey wagon game sees who can tie theirs the fastest, another who can tie theirs correctly the most times in a row. Another idea— some have soaked their hoodie strings in beef broth mixed with illegal, mildly mind-altering chemicals. During extended lock-ups they report that in transport between padded cells, this sustaining concoction kept their revolutionary fervor alive.

Now the question always comes up, front logo or not? We feel that any logo is a good logo and we reserve the right to decide whether the logo of choice or question is in support of our goals or whether we chose it out of protest as it is against our goals. Either way, we always win!

Now the next piece of recommended/required equipment is the ubiquitous backpack.

All of us have been raised with a backpack as a seemingly indispensable component of our child, adolescent, and now adult wardrobe. Never before, however, has what you choose to put in that backpack assumed such a degree of importance and urgency as it now pertains to the successful continuation of the human race. After much research and careful thought, we, your leaders, have decreed that each soldier of the new Progressive Socialist movement must carry with them at all times the following items:

--No less than five copies of the Handbook—always looking for converts!

--5 Herbal Tea bags. For whenever it just gets too tough. Everyone could use a nice Herbal.

--5 homemade energy bars—preferably made from food you scavenged out of a garbage dump.

--one stainless steel water bottle (full).

--a well-hidden copy of parent's credit card #'s-you shouldn't have to bear the full cost of the revolution.

--one extra smart phone battery and charger.

--one Swiss Army knife with instructions for use in 27 languages (California version).

--one copy of Saul Alinsky's <u>Rules for Radicals</u>—fuel for thought!

--one complete color set of magic markers-think Poster Party!

--one waterproof, tear-resistant card listing the toll-free numbers of your nearest ACLU office, the Southern Poverty Law Center, Planned Parenthood, and Black Lives Matter.

--one xl plastic garbage bag-just in case it rains.

--one can of bear repellant—it's a dangerous world out there!

-- one lone ranger mask-no need for explanation here.

The Progressive Guide to Physical and Mental Fitness

You cannot expect to be a loyal and effective member of our army of change if you do not or cannot pay attention to that most rudimentary of responsibilities, always being ready for the fight. As a result, we sincerely encourage you to pay daily attention to the following suggestions:

--Never get out of bed before noon. All loyal soldiers need their rest. If you are going to be out to the wee hours of the morning protesting with or simply regaling friends with stories of protesting, catch up on your rest by sleeping in.

--Always insure an adequate supply of energy drinks. Think of this as the power button on your smart phone. Experience has shown us that these drinks always are more effective when they have been purchased by someone else. Think of it this way, the money you save by not spending on these necessities, you can contribute to the general fund of our movement. Everybody Wins (just like your youth soccer league).

--Practice jumping public transportation turnstiles. Who said being a responsible soldier in the Progressive Army can't be fun? Besides, it makes financial sense. Another Everybody Wins. If your current physical condition prohibits you from such exertion, you can always help out by providing a distraction while someone else performs the jump or simply by shouting words of encouragement like "If you get pinched, we'll call your parents for bail money!"

--Dumpster dive at least once. We have to identify with the underclass. Everybody who is not in the upper class is, by our definition, in the underclass and we know that these poor folks can only eat and survive by scrounging the scraps of the upper-class. For us to have credibility with these homies we have to make them believe that we also walk in their Air Jordans. Taking the dive will give you instant credibility. This will also significantly build up your self-esteem as you now realize that you have "felt their pain." (Thank you, Commander Clinton). A few words of caution: do not swallow or put any retrieved food items into your mouth. Never dive into a dumpster that you cannot climb out of. Always dive with a buddy. Never mess up your official protesting hoodie. Always wear some identifying signage so that everyone knows that you are doing this for the cause. Goggles are always a plus.

--**Chew a Jalapeño pepper every day.** We have to recognize that the energy for our movement can only be sustained through anger. While we cannot fire this up every day, we can fire up intense discomfort. Intense discomfort can be a basis for anger. This is your Zen moment. Channel the discomfort of your mouth and throat into intense hatred for those responsible for you having to chew this pepper. This includes everyone who has anything that you think you have the right to have, anyone enjoying things that you can't enjoy, and anyone who just thinks differently from you. While the pain will eventually pass, the unfairness of your life will not. Always remember, you are entitled to whatever your heart desires.

--**Organize and participate in Progressive Cell meetings.** Basically, these are "feel good" gatherings of you and your cohorts to vent your frustration at the world not accepting your demands for those things you believe you are entitled. These gatherings of like minds must serve to reinforce the belief that everyone's entitlements are equal and therefore justified and must be equally supported. Out of frustration will emerge action, out of action will emerge results. Out of results will emerge power and this is what we are in this for to begin with. Remember we always know better than the non-Progressives what is in their best interest. We know better than they do how to spend their money and we have the right to make these decisions.

Our Motto

"If it is to be, it must be free!" Make sure you have ordered at least two (2) T-shirts for the special price of $19.95 each. One for Saturday and one for Sunday! And let's not forget the Bumper/window sticker promotion:"I'm Left and I'm right; You're Right and you're wrong!", "Left is right, Right is stupid" "Be Left, be right". This assortment can be yours for the unbelievable introductory price of only $9.95.

Our Philosophy

We believe in the fundamental principle that all humans are entitled to an equality of results. That is, despite apparent differences in history, biology, gender, talent and capabilities, all humans should live in a world of material equality based on those with more providing for those with less. While preferring to achieve this through peaceful means, we reserve the right to utilize violence where we deem appropriate in pursuit of our goal of equality. We believe that the only means to this achievement is a strong central, all-powerful world government. We believe in income equality and this can only be achieved through a system of unequal income and resource confiscation with appropriate redistribution. We believe no one has the right to a gun and everyone has the right to a smart phone. We believe in free speech only in the context of safe speech and we reserve the sole right to determine what is safe speech. And finally, we believe we know better than non-Progressives how life should be lived and it is up to us to make it happen.

Tactics to Live By

(These Never Fail)

Cry. Who will prosecute or persecute anyone who is in the throes of tearful grief? It is recommended that the spontaneous tearing up skill be practiced and developed before it is put into play. Please note: this is no longer gender specific.

Shout/Scream but not in unison. This just creates total confusion and our opponents often cannot or will not handle the mayhem. If you get lucky and one of them bops you on the head, just make sure you have a video of it and then sit back. You have just exited on Easy Street!

Chant "Hands Up, Don't Shoot" Never worry about the occasion. This tactic has been known to work when an appropriation of a capitalist's property has taken place and the liberator of said property has been caught. Ignore the legality of any arrest. Simply chanting this seems to quell any desire for prosecution.

Lock arms/sit down and employ one of the above-mentioned verbal renditions.

Refer to a sympathetic celebrity/athlete. It

matters not if the celebrity/athlete mentioned agrees with you or not. Our media friends will hype the celebrity mention and any agreement or disagreement just adds fuel to our fire.

One Final Request

You are the final hope for humanity. Never lose sight of this simple fact. We only have twelve years! Without your determination, involvement, action, and money, civilization as we know it will cease to exist. If you find your determination weakening, and your involvement and action inconvenient, by all means send money. Trust us, it will be much appreciated and we know how to spend it!

We strongly encourage you to purchase and distribute multiple copies of this handbook to your friends, contacts, and total strangers. Our greatest ally is ignorance and this handbook is a solid and reinforcing testimony to this fact. We thank you for your continued support.